UNDERSTANDING DIVINE PROSPERITY

*My towns will again overflow with prosperity,
and the Lord will again comfort Zion and choose Jerusalem.*

Zechariah 1:17 *NIV*

by
Franklin N. Abazie

Understanding Divine Prosperity
COPYRIGHT 2016 BY Franklin N Abazie
ISBN: 978-1-94513310-7

All right reserved. This book or any portion thereof may not be reproduced or used in any manner whatsoever without the express written permission of the publisher, except for the use of brief quotations in a book review. All Bible quotes are from King James Version and others as noted.

Published by: F N ABAZIE PUBLISHING HOUSE—aka, Empowerment Bookstore

That I may publish with the voice of thanksgiving and tell of all thy wondrous works.
Psalms 26:7

To order additional copies, wholesales or booking call:
the Church office (973-372-7518)
or Empowerment Bookstore Hotline (973-393-8518)

Worship address:
343 Sanford Avenue, Newark, New Jersey 07106
Administrative Head Office address:
33 Schley Street Newark New Jersey 07112
Email: pastorfranknto@yahoo.com
Website www.fnabaziehealingministries.org
Publishing House: www.fnabaziepublishinghouse.org

This book is a production of F N Abazie Publishing House. A publication Arms of Miracle of God Ministries 2016.
First Edition

CONTENTS

THE MANDATE OF THE COMMISSION......................iv
ARMS OF THE COMMISSION...................................v
INTRODUCTION...vi
CHAPTER 1
Covenant Prosperity...1
CHAPTER 2
How God Blesses..17
CHAPTER 3
Lasting Success..22
CHAPTER 4
Prayer of Salvation...49
CHAPTER 5
About the Author..61

THE MANDATE OF THE COMMISSION

"The moment is due to impact your world through the revival of the healing & miracle ministry of Jesus Christ of Nazareth.

"I am sending you to restore health unto thee and I will heal thee of thy wounds, said the Lord of Host."

ARMS OF THE COMMISSION

1) F N Abazie Ministries—Miracle of God Ministries (Miracle Chapel Intl)

2) F N Abazie TV Ministries: Global Television Ministry Outreach

3) F N Abazie Radio Ministries: Radio Broadcasting Outreach

4) F N Abazie Publishing House: Book Publication

5) F N Abazie Bible School: also called Word of Healing Bible School (W.O.H.B.S.)

6) F N Abazie Evangelistic Ass: Miracle of God Ministries: Global Crusade

7) Empowerment Bookstore: Book distribution

8) F N Abazie Helping Hands: Meeting the Help of the Needy Worldwide

9) F N Abazie Disaster Recovery Mission: Global Disaster Recovery

10) F N Abazie Prison Ministry: Prison Ministry For All Convicts "Second Chance"

Some of our ministry arms are awaiting the appointed time to commence.

INTRODUCTION

Although I have not always been outspoken on this subject until I read a book from **Glora Copeland** called *God's Will Is Prosperity*, I was not ready to face my critics. Contrary to some assertions, **God's covenant is the platform for all kingdom prosperity.**

Beloved, I wish above all things that thou mayest prosper and be in health, even as thy soul prospereth.
3 John 1:2

Although so many folks that has nothing to do with church and religion has prospered in their life time, through the application of the principles established in the Holy bible. In my own opinion No man or woman can prosper without following the principles and application of the word of God. **Understanding divine prosperity means understanding how God blesses, where God blesses, when God blesses, prosperity in the word of God, the demands of discipline, the place of tithing, fasting and prayers, and, finally, the function of consistency and persistence**.

The blessing of the Lord, it maketh rich, and he addeth no sorrow with it.
Proverbs 10:22

There are so many rich, depressed people all

over the world. Whenever God blesses, it comes sorrow free. It comes with delight, joy and happiness. Divine prosperity is the building block for **lasting success and transgenerational wealth**.

For the love of money is the root of all evil:
which while some coveted after,
they have erred from the faith,
and pierced themselves through with many sorrows.
1 Timothy 6:10

The above scripture talks about the **love of money**. This is one of my favorite quotations about money. You can have MONEY and not LOVE it. And you can love money and not have it. But it is very dangerous to **love money and not have it**.

Most people that **love money** and do not have it end up in misery, in jail or even dead. Contrary to the nagging misconceptions, we will examine why the wicked man prospers and the Godly man doesn't. Every time you apply the covenant of God and its principles, it will work for you.

And I will bless them that bless thee,
and curse him that curseth thee: and in thee
shall all families of the earth be blessed.
Genesis 12:3

God blesses us to establish the integrity of his covenant.

*But thou shalt remember the Lord thy God:
for it is he that giveth thee power to get wealth that he
may establish his covenant which he sware unto
thy fathers, as it is this day.*
Deuternomy 8:18

We are blessed principally to become a blessing to others. Although you may not agree with me, we are blessed primary to become a blessing for the promotion of the **work of the kingdom of God and his righteousness**. Every giver (philanthropist) is a man and a woman who will be wealthy forever. Giving to the poor, the widows, the orphans is important and to impact the world is key—but giving to the church is the access code. *"But seek ye first the kingdom of God, and his righteousness; and all these things shall be added unto you."* (Matthew 6:33)

HAPPY READING!

HIGHLIGHTS

HOW TO PROVOKE THE BLESSINGS OF THE LORD

REPENT

Every time you truly **repent in life**, God is obligated to **restore your life**.

Therefore say thou unto them, Thus saith the Lord of hosts; Turn ye unto me, saith the Lord of hosts, and I will turn unto you, saith the Lord of hosts.
Zechariah 1:3

Peter replied to a question from the crowd—"what shall we do?"—by telling them: *"Repent and be baptized every one of you, in the name of Jesus Christ for the forgiveness of your sins. And you will receive the gift of the Holy Spirit."* (Acts 2:38)

Unless you **repent**, God will not **restore** your life. To be spiritually-minded means to recognize this revelation of scriptures, abundance of material wealth does not guarantee happiness.

The blessing of the Lord, it maketh rich, and he addeth no sorrow with it.
Proverbs 10:22

YOU MUST BE BORN AGAIN

For God so loved the world, that he gave his only begotten Son, that whosoever believeth in him should not perish, but have everlasting life.
John 3:16

    It is very rare for any father to bless a stranger. Every father finds it easy to bless their own biological children. God will only bless and prosper us in life when we genuinely become born again Christians in life. Unless you are born again, you will forever suffer many sorrows in life. Remember—

The blessing of the Lord, it maketh rich, and he addeth no sorrow with it.
Proverbs 10:22

For as many as are led by the Spirit of God, they are the sons of God...
...The Spirit itself beareth witness with our spirit, that we are the children of God: And if children, then heirs; heirs of God, and joint-heirs with Christ; if so be that we suffer with him, that we may be also glorified together.
Romans 8:14, Romans 8:16-17

    Salvation is our sure foundation for any great destiny. *"Nevertheless the foundation of God standeth sure, having this seal, The Lord knoweth them that are his. And, let everyone that nameth the name of Christ depart from iniquity."* (2 Timothy 2:19) So many wealthy people outside of the faith are depressed, angry and dealing with internalized sorrow in the heart.

DECISION

A great man once said, "Decisions are the horses we ride into fame or into shame." *"I call heaven and earth to record this day against you, that I have set before you, life and death, blessing and cursing: therefore choose life that both thou and thy seed may live."* (Deuternomy 30:19)

Decisions are the wheels of destiny. We are free to make our choices in our lifetime—both good and bad. Decisions either takes us into wealth or into abject poverty. We are the total sum of our decisions over a period of time. Our present circumstance, prevailing challenges or success is a product of our decisions.

Our life rotates on the orbit of decision. Joshua said, *"But as for me and my house, we will serve the Lord."* (Joshua 24:15) We must make up our mind to focus on a career that must be productive and rewarding for our lives. We must recognize our calling from God, and follow it through. Lazarus made a choice to eat crumbs.

*And desiring to be fed with the crumbs
which fell from the rich man's table: moreover
the dogs came and licked his sores.*
Luke 16:21

Despite all the riches of his father, the prodigal son took a decision that reduced him to eat the pig's food, until *"he came to himself."* (Luke 15:17) Our lifestyle is a function of our decisions. For example, if you chose to work for someone for $5.00 an hour, there is no way you will become a millionaire in your lifetime. In this life we all have choices to make. There is an opportunity for you to change your mind *today*. Instead of continuing to be an employee of that company, think of starting your own business and employing others to work for you.

PRAYER

But ye beloved, building up your selves on your most holy faith, praying in the Holy Ghost.
Jude 1:20

A prayer-less man is a powerless man or woman. Although divine prosperity demands **covenant pratice**, without a lifestyle of prayer, the believer is doomed. We must all appreciate the place of prayer in our lives. *"Pray without ceasing."* (1 Thessalonians 5:18) In order to access divine prosperity, we must develop a lifestyle of prayer. If you do not communicate to God in prayers, there is no way God will talk to you. Prayer, therefore, is the platform for **all kingdom mysteries and revelations**.

THE WORD OF GOD

Unless otherwise stated, it is the word of God that will give you revelation into the deep things of God. *"The entrance of thy words giveth light; it giveth understanding unto the simple."* (Psalms 119:130) *"But the natural man receiveth not the things of the Spirit of God: for they are foolishness unto him: neither can he know them, because they are spiritually discerned. But he that is spiritual judgeth all things, yet he himself is judged of no man."* (1 Corinthians 2:14-15) To command true and lasting prosperity in life, we must use the word of God to access what and how we need to approach supernatural prosperity.

FAITH IN GOD

Yea, a man may say, Thou hast faith, and I have works: shew me thy faith without thy works, and I will shew thee my faith by my works.
James 2:18

We are admonished in Hebrews that *"without faith it is impossible to please Him."* (Hebrews 11:6) Jesus Christ, see our faith and determine what measure of life favor we merit. *"When Jesus saw their faith..."* (Mark 2:5) We must prove God in all things in life. *"For as the body without the spirit is dead, so faith without works is dead also."* (James 2:26)

SELF DEVELOPMENT & SELF CONFIDENCE

Self-development is a personal obligation for all who aspire to be great in life. After carefully examining the life of Billy Sundays, I concluded that everyone can develop themselves in any calling they choose to in their lifetime. Zig Ziglar once said that any dummy can succeed—if he or she cares to know what it takes to succeed in life.

William "Billy" Sunday (Nov. 19, 1862 – Nov. 6, 1935) was an American athlete who, after being a popular outfielder in baseball's National League during the 1880s, became the most celebrated and influential American evangelist during the first two decades of the 20th century. Born into poverty in Iowa, Sunday spent some years at the Iowa Soldiers' Orphans' Home before working at odd jobs and playing for local running and baseball teams. His speed and agility provided him the opportunity to play baseball in the major leagues for eight years, where he was an average hitter and a good fielder known for his base-running.

Converting to evangelical Christianity in the 1880s, Sunday left baseball for the Christian ministry. He gradually developed his skills as a pulpit evangelist in the Midwest. Then, during the early 20th century, he became the nation's most famous evangelist, with his colloquial sermons and frenetic delivery.

And this is the confidence that we have in him, that,

if we ask any thing according to his will, he heareth us.
1 John 5:14
COVENANT PRACTICE

Although most of us are occupied **praying in the Holy Ghost**, prayer is vital. But until we become a **covenant practitioner**, we are not a candidate for **divine prosperity**. Divine prosperity simply operates on the platform of the "COVENANT OF GOD."

What is the covenant?

While the earth remaineth, seedtime and harvest, and cold and heat, and summer and winter, and day and night shall not cease.
Genesis 8:22

We cannot harvest what we have not sown. So many of us are busy celebrating the anointing. The anointing is good, but it will not guarantee your prosperity in the Kingdom of God.

And why call ye me, Lord, Lord, and do not the things which I say?
Luke 6:46

Most of us are busy shouting Lord, Lord. God hears our cry, but until we provoke his heart, our hand will not handle anything. *"And why call ye me, Lord, Lord, and do not the things which I say?"* (Luke 6:46)

WHY COVENANT PEOPLE MUST PROSPER?

In my own understanding, one of the greatest reasons for covenant wealth is because the seculars and intellectual world—Wall Street and most wealthy people—look down on church religious people. The **poor man** has **no voice** and his **wisdom** is despised everywhere around the world.

> *Now there was found in it a poor wise man,*
> *and he by his wisdom delivered the city;*
> *yet no man remembered that same poor man.*
> *Then said I, Wisdom is better than strength:*
> *nevertheless the poor man's wisdom is despised,*
> *and his words are not heard.*
> **Ecclesiastes 9:15-16**

POVERTY IS A CURSE IN MY OWN SCRIPTURAL INTERPRETATION

Although **poverty is a curse**, this curse was broken on the cross. Besides **deliverance from sin and sickness and redemption of our soul**, if you are a poor man or woman in life—*"Christ hath redeemed us from the curse of the law, being made a curse for us: for it is written, Cursed is every one that hangeth on a tree: That the blessing of Abraham might come on the Gentiles through Jesus Christ; that we might receive the promise of the Spirit through faith."* (Galatians 3:13-14)

We have little or no alternative in life as a poor

man/woman. *"My family is poor in Manasseh, and I am the least in my father's house."* (Judges 6:15)

WEALTH GIVES THE BELIEVER
A VOICE IN HIS OR HER COMMUNITY

Unless you are in command of wealth—you are rich and wealthy—nobody cares to listen or to hear from you. Wealth has many friends and it attracts attention from everyone in life. (See Proverbs 19:4.) Whether or not you disagree with me, the fact is that rich folks will forever rule over poor people. *"The rich ruleth over the poor, and the borrower is servant to the lender."* (Proverbs 22:7)

Although wealth has so many friends, you will agree with me that **Donald Trump** is doing well in the **presidnetial campaign** and making so much **imapct** because the guy, as a billionaire, attracts so many people and draws so much attention from the media.

WEALTH GUARANTEES
BOLDNESS & AUTHORITY

Wealth grants **strength and power**. Besides commanding authority and boldness, every rich man or woman is highly respected in every society.

WEALTH LEAVES US WITH
SO MANY OPTIONS

Every poor man or woman has few alternatives. But the rich man has plenty of alternatives in life. I remember a rich man in Lagos, Nigeria, who, every time his wife gets pregnant, he sends her to America to deliver their child. *"But money answereth all things."* (Ecclesiastes 10:19)

> *Wealth maketh many friends;*
> *but the poor is separated from his neighbour.*
> **Proverbs 19:4**

But remember, *"The rich and poor meet together: the Lord is the maker of them all."* (Proverbs 22:2)

It is written, *"For there is no difference between the Jew and the Greek: for the same Lord over all is rich unto all that call upon him."* (Romans 10:12)

We must, therefore, make a conscious effort not only to be comfortable, but to also make an impact as a blessing to our generation and the future generations to come. "We must aspire to acquire the desires—**wealth**—we admire."

HIS DESTINY WAS THE CROSS…

HIS PURPOSE WAS LOVE…

HIS REASON WAS YOU…

REPEAT THIS LOUDLY:

**I must get wealth
by all genuine means in my lifetime.**

For ye know the grace of our Lord Jesus Christ, that, though he was rich, yet for your sakes he became poor, that ye through his poverty might be rich.
2 Corinthians 8:9

THE RESOURCE OF COVENANT WEALTH

GOD

He that hath pity upon the poor lendeth unto the Lord; and that which he hath given will he pay him again.
Proverbs 19:17

He that giveth unto the poor shall not lack: but he that hideth his eyes shall have many a curse.
Proverbs 28:27

We must prove our **love** for **Jesus Christ** by our **giving**. (Liberality) *"The liberal soul shall be made fat: and he that watereth shall be watered also himself."* (Proverbs 11:25) *"But seek ye first the kingdom of God, and his righteousness; and all these things shall be added unto you."* (Matthew 6:33)

DECISION

Although we totally depend on God, the decisions over the affairs of our life are our sole responsibility. The **heart** is the platform to be **wealthy and poor**. For you and me to be successful in life, we must have thought about it, reflected on it, planned it, programmed it in our lifetime and earned it. (Made it.) We must decide in life if we must be wealthy or poor in life.

DESIRE IT

Lazarus desired eating crumbs as a beggar. Riches are good and they make life easy. Therefore we must desire prosperity (wealth and material riches) in our lifetime. Oftentimes we, out of neglect and ignorance, desire to be beggars in life.

*And desiring to be fed with the crumbs
which fell from the rich man's table:
moreover the dogs came and licked his sores.*
Luke 16:21

PRAYER POINT TO PROVOKE DIVINE PROSPERITY

—Lord, grant me the power of getting wealth and establish your sovereignity, in the name of Jesus Christ.

—I paralyze any contrary power, manipulating my finances, in Jesus mighty name.

—I demolish and abolish all strongholds of poverty in my life and family, in the name of Jesus Christ.

—Lord, I desire your kingdom and your righteousness.

—I rebuke and destroy out all spirits of the cankerworm, palmerworm, caterpillar, and locust that would eat up my blessings in the name of Jesus. (Joel 2:25)

—Lord Jesus, you teach me to profit and lead me in the way I should go. (Isaiah 48:17)

—You are Jehovah-Jireh my provider. (Genesis 22:14)

—You are El Shaddai, the God who is more than enough.

—Wealth and riches are in my house, because I fear You and delight greatly in Your commandments— **your word**. (Psalms 112:1-3)

—The blessing of the Lord upon my life makes me rich and He adds no sorrow with it.

—I am blessed coming in and blessed going out, blessed in the city and everywhere I go.

—I am God's servant and He takes pleasure in my prosperity because I favor His righteous cause. (Psalms 35:27)

—Jesus Christ, You became poor, that through Your poverty I am made rich. (2 Corinthians 8:9)

—I meditate in the word day and night and whatever I do prospers, in the name of Jesus. (Psalms 1:3)

—Peace is within my walls and prosperity within my palace. (Psalms 122:7-8)

—I prosper through the prophets and prophetic ministry. (Ezra 6:14)

—I believe the true prophets of God and I prosper, in the name of Jesus. (2 Chronicles 20:20)

—I am your servant, Lord, thank You for prospering me. (Nehemiah 1:11)

—The God of heaven prospers me. (Nehemiah 2:20)

—I live in the prosperity of the King. (Jeremiah 23:5)

—Through Your favor Lord, I am a prosperous person. (Genesis 39:2)

—Lord, You called me and You make my way prosperous, daily. (Isaiah 48:15)

—I pray and fast in secret and You reward me openly. (Matthew 6:6, 18)

—I am rewarded because I trust You and diligently seek You. (Hebrews 11:6)

—Lord, You have released the wealth of the wicked into my hands, in the name of Jesus.

—Lord, I thank You that, You have brought me into my wealthy place. (Psalms 66:12)

—I give and it is given to me, good measure, pressed down, shaken together and running over. (Luke 6:38)

—The floodgates of heaven are open over my life and I receive more than I have enough room to receive. (Malachi 3:10)

—There are no holes in my bag, in the name of Jesus.

—The devourer is rebuked and his assignment is cancelled, for my sake in the name of Jesus. (Malachi 3:11)

—All nations call me blessed and I am a delightful land. (Malachi 3:12)

—I am in league with the stones of the field. (Job 5:23)

—My gates are open so that the wealth of the nations comes into my life continually, in the name of Jesus. (Isaiah 60:11)

—Your showers of blessing are upon my life. (Ezekial 34:26)

—My vats overflow continually, in the name of Jesus. (Joel 2:24).

—My barns are filled with plenty and my presses burst with new wine. (Proverbs 3:10)

—You have commanded Your blessing upon my storehouses, O Lord. (Deuteronomy 28:8)

—My barns are full and overflowing, my sheep bring forth thousands and ten thousands, my oxen are strong to labor. (Psalms 144:13-14)

—The plowman overtakes the reaper in my life and the treader of grapes, the sower of the seed and I live in continual harvest in the name of Jesus. (Amos 9:13)

—My floor is full of wheat and my vats overflow with wine and oil. (Joel 2:25)

—You have dealt wondrously with me, I eat and am satisfied. (Joel 2:26)

—You lead me into the land flowing with milk and honey, O Lord. (Exodus 3:8)

—You have brought me into a land without scarceness or lack, thank you, Lord Jesus. (Deuteronomy 8:9)

—All grace abounds toward me because I have all sufficiency in all things and abound to every good work. (2 Corinthians 9:8)

—My head is anointed with oil and my cup runs over. (Psalms 23:5)

—I have riches and honor in abundance. (2 Chronicles 18:1)

—The rock pours out rivers of oil. (Job 29:6)

—My feet are dipped in oil. (Deuternomy 33:24)

—I love wisdom, I inherit substance and my treasures are filled at all times, in the name of Jesus. (Proverbs 8:18)

—Lord, You have brought honey out of the rock for me in the name of Jesus. (Psalms 81:16)

—I have plenty of silver, in the name of Jesus (Job 28:1)

—Your river of life leads me to gold, in the name of Jesus. (Genesis 2:11-12)

—I inherit the land. (Psalms 37:29)

—I refuse to allow the angel of blessing to depart without blessing me, in the name of Jesus. (Genesis 2:6)

CHAPTER 1
COVENANT PROSPERITY

Among the bugging questions about kingdom prosperity is the criticism and prevailing sarcasms of church folks. Growing up as a young man, the famous quote, **"As poor as church rats,"** for a long time prevailed among the generation before me, as far as I can remember. Prosperity theology has been condemned and strongly opposed, yet the promotion of the church of GOD depends heavily upon it.

But thou shalt remember the Lord thy God:
for it is he that giveth thee power to get wealth
that he may establish his covenant which
he sware unto thy fathers, as it is this day
Deuteronomy 8:18

In this era, reality theology and prosperity theology have come to a merging point. The work of GOD depends on the prosperity of the church. I rented a place on Sanford Avenue in Newark, New Jersey, but I was forced to relocate quickly because I could not keep up with the rent of the facility. Anyone who tells you that GOD does not need the church to prosper should come and ask me directly. The reason for

SAVATION was not just for the deliverance from sin and sickness—it is also for deliverance from the plague of poverty, so that we can richly enjoy our lives as long as we live here on Earth.

Charge them that are rich in this world, that they be not highminded, nor trust in uncertain riches, but in the living God, who giveth us richly all things to enjoy.
1 Timothy 6:17-19

That they do good, that they be rich in good works, ready to distribute, willing to communicate; For ye know the grace of our Lord Jesus Christ, that, though he was rich, yet for your sakes he became poor, that ye through his poverty might be rich
2 Corinthians 8:9

Among the reasons Jesus Christ came was to restore us with prosperity—*"I am come that they might have life, and that they might have it more abundantly."* (John 10:10) Although some of us are privileged to be born from wealthy parents, no man was born to be poor in life, neither was any woman born to be poor. Poverty and riches are the choice we make in life—either voluntarily or involuntary. *"For there is no difference between the Jew and the Greek: for the same Lord over all is rich unto all that call upon him."* (Romans 10:12)

PROSPERITY in the KINGDOM OF GOD does not answer to PRAYER and FASTING, it does not respond to the mysteries of the PROPHETIC.

GOD's PROSPERITY is provoked only on the platform of the covenant. *"While the earth remaineth, seedtime and harvest, and cold and heat, and summer and winter, and day and night shall not cease."* (Genesis 8:22)

Thus saith the Lord; If ye can break my covenant of the day, and my covenant of the night, and that there should not be day and night in their season; Then may also my covenant be broken with David my servant, that he should not have a son to reign upon his throne; and with the Levites the priests, my ministers.
Jeremiah 33:20-21

As long as we understand the covenant of GOD, GOD is obligated to respond to us on the flat form of the covenant. *"Thus saith the Lord; If my covenant be not with day and night, and if I have not appointed the ordinances of heaven and earth; Then will I cast away the seed of Jacob and David my servant, so that I will not take any of his seed to be rulers over the seed of Abraham, Isaac, and Jacob: for I will cause their captivity to return, and have mercy on them."* (Jeremiah 33:25-26)

Remember—*"My covenant will I not break, nor alter the thing that is gone out of my lips."* (Psalms 89:34)

WHAT IS THE COVENANT?

In my interpretation, a covenant is an agreement, a vow and a contract built by GOD on well-defined terms, sealed with an oath. As long as we are committed to do our portion of the contract, GOD is obligated to meet his covenant promised to us.

Hebrews tells us, *"For men verily swear by the greater: and an oath for confirmation is to them an end of all strife. Wherein God, willing more abundantly to shew unto the heirs of promise the immutability of his counsel, confirmed it by an oath: That by two immutable things, in which it was impossible for God to lie, we might have a strong consolation, who have fled for refuge to lay hold upon the hope set before us."* (Hebrews 6:16-18)

WHAT IS PROSPERITY?

Prosperity is the state of flourishing, thriving, good fortune or successful social status. Prosperity often encompasses wealth, but also includes other factors which can be independent of wealth to varying degrees—such as happiness and health. GOD HAS COMMANDED US TO GET MONEY THROUGH THE RIGHT ETHICAL AND MORAL WAY.

As the partridge sitteth on eggs, and hatcheth them not;
so he that getteth riches, and not by right,
shall leave them in the midst of his days,
and at his end shall be a fool.
Jeremiah 17:11

MOST WORLD-KNOWN FAMOUS AND GREAT MEN WERE MEN OF RICHES...and strong men retain riches. *"The rich man's wealth is his strong city: the destruction of the poor is their poverty."* (Proverbs 18:11)

WE MUST ALL BE DETERMINED TO ACQUIRE WEALTH BY ALL GENUINE MEANS POSSIBLE—MORALLY AND ETHICALLY.

WHAT IS SIN?

In the German interpretation of sin, the word "debt" is interpreted as sin. If you are living in debt, you are literally living in sin. We are commanded in scriptures—

For the Lord thy God blesseth thee, as he promised thee: and thou shalt lend unto many nations, but thou shalt not borrow; and thou shalt reign over many nations, but they shall not reign over thee.
Deuteronomy 15:6

On the prevailing subject of "DIVINE PROSPERITY," the above scripture establishes that we must not borrow in our lifetime. Every time you operate outside of the commandment of God, you are committing sin. *"He that committeth sin is of the devil; for the devil sinneth from the beginning. For this purpose the son of God was manifested that he might destroy the works of the devil."* (1 John 3:8)

He that covereth his sins shall not prosper: but whoso confesseth and forsaketh them shall have mercy.
Proverbs 28:13

We live in a very sinful generation, in a time where the evil man is prospering. Fret not thyself because of evildoers, neither be thou envious against the workers of iniquity.

Despite what David said in Psalms 51:3—*"For I acknowledge my transgressions and my sin is ever before me."* We must not take the purpose of the coming life and death of Jesus in vain. Man's nature was born in sin like David attested. *"Behold I was shapen in iniquity; and in sin did my mother conceive me."* (Psalms 51:5)

WHO IS A SINNER?

Although everyone that is covetous is a sinner, GOD made it clear to us in the Holy bible—*"But godliness with contentment is great gain."* (1 Timothy 6:6) *"For what shall it profit a man, if he shall gain the whole world, and lose his own soul? Or what shall a man give in exchange for his soul?"* (Mark 8:36-37)

On the subject of who is a sinner, there is no exemption—everyone is included. It's time to tell yourself the truth. Is there any hidden sinful lifestyle you are dealing with? Confess it and crush it in the open with prayers.

Examine yourselves, whether ye be in the faith; prove your own selves. Know ye not your own selves, how that Jesus Christ is in you, except ye be reprobates?
2 Corinthians 13:5

Although most faith people live in denial about the work of the flesh, from my own scriptural understanding, everyone operating within the scope of Galatians 5:20-21 is classified as a sinner.

Now the works of the flesh are manifest, which are these; Adultery, fornication, uncleanness, lasciviousness, idolatry, witchcraft, hatred, variance, emulations, wrath, strife, seditions, heresies, envyings, murders, drunkenness, revellings, and such like: of the which I tell you before, as I have also told you in time past, that they which do such things shall not inherit the kingdom of God.
Galatians 5:20-21

Further supporting scripture...

But the fearful, and unbelieving, and the abominable, and murderers, and whoremongers, and sorcerers, and idolaters, and all liars, shall have their part in the lake which burneth with fire and brimstone: which is the second death.
Revelation 21:8

WHO, THEREFORE, IS A SINNER?

1) The Lazy Man: It is sinful for any able body man/woman to fold their hand and make themselves beggars. The Bible says, *"the sluggard will not plow by reason of the cold; therefore shall he beg in harvest, and have nothing."* (Proverbs 20:4) In my understanding, laziness is a sin. *"For even when we were with you, this we commanded you, that if any would not work, neither should he eat."* (2 Thessalonians 3:10) \

Covenant mentality demands that we all understand that God has done His part over our lives. Jesus said I must work. It is dignified for every believer to earn money through the work of their hands.

Although most lazy people live in denial and tend to blame someone else, nevertheless, Godliness demands that we take absolute responsibility for the outcome of our lives.

2) Unbelievers: In my view, all that have not acknowledged Jesus Christ as Lord and savior are sinners. The Bible says *God heareth not sinners*. Without contradiction, all unbelievers live in a sinful lifestyle. Unless God has mercy, most unbelievers will not make eternity in heaven.

3) Liars: *"All liars, shall have their part in the lake which burneth with fire and brimstone: which is the second death."* (Revelation 21:8) Someone whom I know very well lies so much to themselves, they became a beggar by paralyzing their future and frustrating the will of God over their life.

HOW DO I COME OUT OF SIN?

Know ye not, that to whom ye yield yourselves servants to obey, his servants ye are to whom ye obey; whether of sin unto death, or of obedience unto righteousness
Romans 6:16

You must *REPENT*, *CONFESS* and *PROCLAIM* the LORD JESUS CHRIST. The word says as many as received him, to them gave He power to become the sons of God. Even to them that believe on his name.

To qualify for divine visitation, do the following (with sincerity):

1) *Acknowledge* that you are a sinner and that He died for you. (Romans 3:23)

2) *Repent of your sins.* (Acts 3:19, Luke 13:5, 2 Peter 3:9)

3) *Believe in your heart* that Jesus died for your sin. (Romans 10:10)

4) *Confess Jesus as the Lord over your life.* (Romans 10:10, Acts 2:21)

Now repeat this Prayer after me—

Say Lord Jesus, I accept you today, as my Lord and my savior, forgive me of my sins wash me with your blood. Right now, I believe, I am sanctified, I am save, I am free, I am free from the Power of sin to serve the Lord Jesus. Thank you Lord for saving me. Amen.

Congratulations.

YOU ARE NOW A BORN AGAIN CHRISTIAN!

STEPS TO OVERCOME THE LIFESTYLE OF SIN

FAITH

No one will overcome a sinful lifestyle without faith. Faith is the catalyst that will push us out of sin. Most prevailing SINFUL HABITS will not stop overnight—unless the spirit of faith takes over our willpower to yield to SIN. Unless we develop faith, SINFUL HABITS have the power to prevail.

DECISION

Decisions are the gateway into our freedom, liberty and a glorious future. When we settle for less, we can only get what is entitled for the less privileged.

(See Luke 16:21.) "Despite all the riches of the father, the prodigal son took a drastic decision that reduced him to eat the pig's food, until he came to himself." (Luke 15:17) At some point in our lifetime, WE made certain DECISIONS that were detrimental to our future. Decisions are like wheels—we either ride into FAME or SHAME in life.

PRAYER

Every man of PRAYER is a man/woman of SPIRITUAL ABUNDANCE. "The sleep of a labouring man is sweet, whether he eat little or much: but the abundance of the rich will not suffer him to sleep." Prayer brings assurance that regardless of the circumstances, the believers believe it will get better. We must always depend on the Holy Spirit in Prayers.

HOW TO ACTIVATE THE HOLY SPIRIT IN YOUR LIFE

First of all, you must believe that there is a Holy Spirit.

1) *Acknowledge* the person of the Holy Spirt.

2) *Believe* in the ministration of the Holy Spirit.

3) *Submit & obey* the person of the Holy Spirit.

4) *Welcome* the sweet presence of the Holy Spirit.

Begin a relationship with the Holy Spirit today and make Him your best friend. Never start your day without inviting the person of the Holy Spirit to come into your life.

SUMMARY OF CHAPTER ONE

A covenant is a deal enacted by God, based on well-defined terms and sealed with an oath. The Old and New Testament simply mean the Old and New Covenant. Our portion is to access the covenants of God on every issue of interest to us, including the covenant of prosperity. (Hebrews 6:13-18)

The covenant is superior to all prevailing economic situations and circumstances because it is God's bailout instrument from ALL harsh economic situations. That means economic hardships—famine and drought cannot stop it (Psalms 33:18-19, 37:18-19, 91:1-7)

However, for us to access the blessings of financial fortune as received by the prophets of old, we must walk in their steps to command the same order of financial fortune that they commanded. It is following the steps of giants that make giants. The Bible admonishes us to *"be not slothful, but followers of them who through faith and patience inherit the promises."* (Hebrews 6:12) Thus, there is no shortcut to a world of financial fortune—it is engaging in covenant practice that empowers us to prevail in hard times. (Malachi 3:10-18, 4:1-4)

Wealth gotten by vanity shall be diminished: but he that gathereth by labour shall increase.
Proverbs 13:11

We must all understand that wealth gotten by vanity shall be diminished: but he that gathereth by labour shall increase. Outside of the KINGDOM OF GOD, someone said look for a business or a trade to serve a crowd of people and you will be very rich.

Even as we aspire to get wealth, we must remember that we must make HEAVEN AT LAST WITH JESUS CHRIST IN ETERNITY. *"For what shall it profit a man, if he shall gain the whole world, and lose his own soul? Or what shall a man give in exchange for his soul? Whosoever therefore shall be ashamed of me and of my words in this adulterous and sinful generation; of him also shall the Son of man be ashamed, when he cometh in the glory of his Father with the holy angels."* (Mark 8:36-38)

WHAT AM I SAYING?

We must pursue DIVINE PROSPERITY with a consciousness of making the KINGDOM OF GOD AT LAST. So many good church people ended up in ritual killing and all sorts of human and diabolic sacrifices just to make more money to survive. *"For what shall it profit a man, if he shall gain the whole world, and lose his own soul? Or what shall a man give in exchange for his soul?"*

DECISION KEYS

1) Nothing changes until you make up your mind.

2) Decision is the gateway to deliverance.

3) Until you decide, no one will decide for you.

4) Your prosperity is proportional to your decisions.

5) The decision you make will determine the future you will create

6) Decision creates future and fulfills destinies.

7) Decision beautifies our future.

8) Decision keeps you out of trouble.

9) Decision exempts you from evil.

10) Decision gurantees eternity.

11) You can only go far in life by your faith decisions.

12) You are poor because you made such decisions

13) Make a decision and change your life.

14) Life changing decisions are a function of quality

information.

15) Success in life is a function of decision.

16) Life experiences are full of decisions.

17) Decisions change destinies.

18) Never settle for information—always look for revelation.

19) You are where you are today based on your last decision.

20) Information is crucial in decision making.

21) Decision makers rule the world.

22) You can rule your world with quality decisions.

23) As long as you decide rightly, Satan cannot harrass you.

BORN AGAIN

*Jesus answered and said unto him, Verily, verily,
I say unto thee, Except a man be born again,
he cannot see the kingdom of God. Nicodemus saith unto
him, How can a man be born when he is old?
can he enter the second time into his mother's womb,
and be born? Jesus answered, Verily, verily, I say unto
thee, Except a man be born of water and of the Spirit,
he cannot enter into the kingdom of God. That which is
born of the flesh is flesh; and that which is born of the
Spirit is spirit. Marvel not that I said unto thee,
Ye must be born again. The wind bloweth where it
listeth, and thou hearest the sound thereof,
but canst not tell whence it cometh, and whither it
goeth: so is every one that is born of the Spirit.*
John 3:3-8

CHAPTER 2

HOW GOD BLESSES

So Abram departed, as the Lord had spoken unto him; and Lot went with him: and Abram was seventy and five years old when he departed out of Haran.
Genesis 12:4

GOD blesses us among other channels through: DIVINE DIRECTION, DIVINE IDEAS, DIVINE FAVOR, HARD WORK.

DIVINE DIRECTION

Our giving first into the KINGDOM OF GOD provokes, besides other mysteries, DIVINE DIRECTION. It is DIVINE DIRECTION that sets the pace for SUPERNATURAL PROSPERITY. Every time we follow GOD'S leading, we are heading into supernatural abundance. GOD directs us into our own blessing. *"Thus saith the Lord, thy Redeemer, the Holy One of Israel; I am the Lord thy God which teacheth thee to profit, which leadeth thee by the way that thou shouldest go."* (Isaiah 48:17)

IF WE MUST UNDERSTAND DIVINE PROSPERITY, WE MUST EXPLORE DIVINE IDEAS CONCERNING OUR LIVES.

DIVINE IDEAS

By reason of DIVINE WISDOM OF GOD, we are obligated to operate under the platform of DIVINE IDEAS. *"The Lord by wisdom hath founded the earth; by understanding hath he established the heavens."* (Proverbs 3:19) GOD gave us our brilliant mind to think, mediate, innovate and create new things. A wise man once said, "if you can think well, you will come out of trouble." Another man said, "wisdom is our ability to think well." Jacob, through Divine ideas, escaped slavery from the house of Laban. (See Genesis 30:26-31.)

Divine ideas made these few young men what they are today. Mark Zuckerberg, who started Facebook, and Travis Kalanick are among the richest young men in their generation. Travis Cordell Kalanick is an American entrepreneur. He is the co-founder of the peer-to-peer file sharing company Red Swoosh and the transportation network company Uber. In 2014, he entered the Forbes list of the 400 richest Americans at position #290, with an estimated net worth of $6 billion. Mark Elliot Zuckerberg is an American computer programmer, Internet entrepreneur and philanthropist. He is the chairman, chief executive and co-founder of the social networking website Facebook. His net worth is estimated to be $48.2 billion as of 2016.

DIVINE FAVOR
GOD blesses our lives through DIVINE FAVOR. The Holy Spirit grants us supernatural favor to

obtain help from men of strategic influential positions in life. We get help and access to either finances, or we get an offer for a salaried well-paying job. Divine favor will change anyone's story anywhere in the world.

EXAMPLES OF GOD'S HELP FROM THE BIBLE

THE CHILDREN OF ISREAL GOT HELP FROM GOD AGAINST THE EGYPTIANS

"And I will give this people favour in the sight of the Egyptians: and it shall come to pass, that, when ye go, ye shall not go empty." (Exodus 3:21) The children of Isreal were delivered from the bondage of the EGYPTIANS and became a prosperous people by the favor of GOD.

JOSEPH

Although Joseph was destined to be great, he got the help of GOD through man. As a SLAVE in POTIPOHAR'S HOUSE, Joseph got the help of GOD. *"And the Lord was with Joseph, and he was a prosperous man; and he was in the house of his master the Egyptian."* (Genesis 39:2) As a prisoner, JOSEPH got the help of GOD. *"But the Lord was with Joseph, and shewed him mercy, and gave him favour in the sight of the keeper of the prison."* (Genesis 39:21)

Joseph became a PRIME MINISTER by the help of GOD. Apostle Paul said, *"Having therefore obtained help of God, I continue unto this day, witnessing both to small and great, saying none other things than those which the prophets and Moses did say should come."* (Acts 26:22)

HOW DO I GET DIVINE FAVOR?

WE MUST SHOW OTHER PEOPLE FAVOR IF WE ARE TO RECEIVE FAVOR. We must FAVOR everyone every time we who are in power and we have the opportunity to do it. *"Withhold not good from them to whom it is due, when it is in the power of thine hand to do it. Say not unto thy neighbour, Go, and come again, and to morrow I will give; when thou hast it by thee."* (Proverbs 3:27-28) It is written, *"He that diligently seeketh good procureth favour: but he that seeketh mischief, it shall come unto him."* (Proverbs 11:27)

WE MUST GO TO THE THRONE ROOM OF PRAYERS TO OBTAIN DIVINE FAVOR. *"Let us therefore come boldly unto the throne of grace, that we may obtain mercy, and find grace to help in time of need."* (Hebrews 4:16)

HARD WORK

WE MUST BE HARD WORKING PEOPLE. JESUS said, *"I must work the works of him that sent me, while it is day: the night cometh, when no man can work."* (JOHN 9:4)

WE MUST BE DETERMINED TO SUCCEED IN LIFE.

SUMMARY OF CHAPTER 2

—We must depend first on God.

—We must believe in ourselves.

—We must favor everyone when it is in our power to do so.

—We must be determined in life to work towards excellence.

—We must put in extra effort in all we do in life.

—We must search out for divine ideas, divine direction and vision.

CHAPTER 3
LASTING SUCCESS

This book of the law shall not depart out of thy mouth; but thou shalt meditate therein day and night, that thou mayest observe to do according to all that is written therein: for then thou shalt make thy way prosperous, and then thou shalt have good success.
Joshua 1:8

WHAT IS LASTING SUCCESS?

By "lasting success," I literally mean transgenerational wealth, health and longevity in families.

Wealth gotten by vanity shall be diminished: but he that gathereth by labour shall increase.
Proverbs 13:11

We are assured by the Holy bible that *"God is able to make all grace abound toward you; that ye, always having all sufficiency in all things, may abound to every good work."* (2 Corinthians 9:8). We must realize from scriptures that lasting success is our heritage in Christ. Every child of God is a candidate for transgenerational wealth, long life and good health. It is written, *"With long life will I satisfy him, and shew him my salvation."* (Psalms 91:16)

It is also written, *"Worthy is the Lamb that was*

slain to receive power, and riches, and wisdom, and strength, and honour, and glory, and blessing." (Revelation 5:12)

This establishes that redemption is our gateway to lasting success in life. However, God empowers us for lasting wealth through the revelation and application of the covenant. This implies operating within the established covenant secrets in the Word that launches people into lasting success—with good health, abundance of wealth and long life.

Although we all want to be SUCCESSFUL in life, no one can empower himself for lasting success in life. It is only possible by the help of the ALMIGHTY GOD. Until GOD empowers us, we are utterly powerless. We must therefore recognize that we can only commit to GOD on His own terms, not ours. That is—there is always a part we must play before we can commit God to His part. In my scriptural understanding, it is the revelation of the terms of the covenant that transforms men and women into the realms of inexplicable and undeniable success in life.

WHAT IS A COVENANT?

A covenant is a deal enacted by God, based on well-defined terms and sealed with an oath. As we all know, the Bible is a book of covenants. The Old and New Testament simply mean the Old and New Covenant, and revelation is about accessing the covenants of God on every issue of interest to us—including the covenant of prosperity and lasting success.

But thou shalt remember the Lord thy God:
for it is he that giveth thee power to get wealth,
that he may establish his covenant which he sware
unto thy fathers, as it is this day.
Deuteronomy 8:18

The covenant of GOD is superior to all prevailing economic situations and circumstances. It is God's bailout instrument from ALL detrimental economic circumstances. That means economic hardships, famine and drought cannot stop it. (Psalms 33:18-19, 37:18-19)

WHAT, THEN, IS THE COVENANT OF LASTING SUCCESS?

As long as you are not a giver, you will forever experience hardship and frustration in life. The Bible says that, *"the liberal soul shall be made fat."* (Proverbs 11:25) Lasting success operates on the platform of the covenant of seedtime and harvest. It is written: *"While the earth remaineth, seedtime and harvest, and cold and heat, and summer and winter, and day and night shall not cease."* (Genesis 8:22) 'Seedtime' and 'harvest' meaning giving and receiving, which provide the gateway to acquire divine prosperity in life—GOD's KIND OF PROSPERITY.

However, we need the understanding of "GIVING GRACE" to sustain an ever-growing giving life.

Concerning the Macedonian Church, the Bible says: *"How that in a great trial of affliction the abundance of their joy and their deep poverty abounded unto the riches of their liberality. For to their power, I bear record, yea, and beyond their power they were willing of themselves; Therefore, as ye abound in every thing, in faith, and utterance, and knowledge, and in all diligence, and in your love to us, see that ye abound in this grace also."* (2 Corinthians 8:2-3, 7; see also Philippians 4:15-19; John 10:17-18.)

HOW STRONG IS THIS COVENANT?

"Thus saith the Lord; If ye can break my covenant of the day, and my covenant of the night, and that there should not be day and night in their season; Then may also my covenant be broken with David my servant, that he should not have a son to reign upon his throne; and with the Levites the priests, my ministers. Thus saith the Lord; If my covenant be not with day and night, and if I have not appointed the ordinances of heaven and earth; Then will I cast away the seed of Jacob, and David my servant, so that I will not take any of his seed to be rulers over the seed of Abraham, Isaac, and Jacob: for I will cause their captivity to return, and have mercy on them."

That means that as long as the day and night keep exchanging position and the sun and moon continue to rule the day and night, all of God's covenants in the Bible remain active and progressively forceful. Besides GOD's covenant of protection, healing, and deliverance, the covenant of financial prosperity is provoked only by us—when we give willingly. Among other channels to provoke the covenant are: when we give to the poor, the orphans, when we pay our tithes and worship GOD with an offering as part of the church service. As long as we do our portion of GOD's covenant obligation, GOD is committed to keep HIS part of the deal. *"My covenant will I not break, nor alter the thing that is gone out of my lips."* (Psalms 89:34)

WHAT ARE GOD'S COVENANT REQUIREMENTS FOR DIVINE PROSPERITY?

TITHING

Tithing is the foundational pillar for all who aspire to be prosperous in life. As long as we do not tithe, "our life is bound to be tither." It is written: *"Bring ye all the tithes into the storehouse, that there may be meat in mine house, and prove me now herewith, saith the Lord of hosts, if I will not open you the windows of heaven, and pour you out a blessing, that there shall not be room enough to receive it."* (Malachi 3:10; Leviticus 27:30)

It is also written: *"Honour the Lord with thy substance, and with the firstfruits of all thine increase: So shall thy barns be filled with plenty, and thy presses shall burst out with new wine."* (Proverbs 3:9-10)

For God so loved the world, that he gave his only begotten Son, that whosoever believeth in him should not perish, but have everlasting life.
John 3:16

All givers never lack. *"He that giveth unto the poor shall not lack."* (Proverbs 28:27) All financial testimonies in the body of Christ are rooted in consistent tithing, giving to the poor and the orphans—helping the needy world-wide.

For instance, Abraham was a tither, he became possessor of heaven and earth. For us to access the blessings of Abraham, we must do the works of Abraham. Remember, Christ redeemed us from the curse of the law to connect us to the blessings of Abraham. All we need to do is walk in his steps to flow in the kind of blessings that he experienced. (Genesis 14:19-20; John 8:39; Galatians 3:13-14, 29) Thus, tithing remains a covenant obligation to all that desire DIVINE PROSPERITY IN LIFE.

Some in the secular world argue and criticize about TITHING. But our tithe is not a donation. Rather, it is part of our spiritual responsibilities. The truth is, any believer who is not a tither will remain a financial struggler. It is impossible to be in command of financial prosperity without the virtue of liberality—the act and practice of GIVING to the poor, the church and to the prophet of GOD.

GIVING TO JESUS CHRIST & THE KINGDOM OF GOD

Every time we give grudgingly and sparingly, we lose the SPIRITUAL PRIVILAGE and FINANCIAL REWARD of the ritual of GIVING. *"But this I say, He which soweth sparingly shall reap also sparingly;*

and he which soweth bountifully shall reap also bountifully. Every man according as he purposeth in his heart, so let him give; not grudgingly, or of necessity: for God loveth a cheerful giver." (2 Corinthians 9:6-7)

GIVING to THE KINGDOM OF GOD is for the expansion, promotion and advancement of the church of Jesus Christ. Although so many of us misinterpret and misrepresent "GIVING" to the pastor and the church of God as a donation—GIVING MONEY TO GOD IS NOT A DONATION. "*A man can receive nothing, except it be given him from heaven."* (John 3:27)

There is nothing sufficient enough that we can give to GOD, our creator—*"for without me ye can do nothing."* (John 15:5)

The Bible attested:

Hear, O my people, and I will speak; O Israel, and I will testify against thee: I am God, even thy God. I will not reprove thee for thy sacrifices or thy burnt offerings, to have been continually before me. I will take no bullock out of thy house, nor he goats out of thy folds. For every beast of the forest is mine, and the cattle upon a thousand hills. I know all the fowls of the mountains: and the wild beasts of the field are mine. If I were hungry, I would not tell thee: for the world is mine, and the fulness thereof. Will I eat the flesh of bulls, or drink the blood of goats? Offer unto God thanksgiving; and pay thy vows unto the most High: And call upon me in the day of trouble: I will deliver thee, and thou shalt glorify me.
Psalms 50:7-15

"GIVING" to the church of GOD is a kingdom obligation that cannot be NEGLECTED nor IGNORED. It is written: *"Ye shall kindle no fire throughout your habitations upon the sabbath day. And Moses spake unto all the congregation of the children of Israel, saying, This is the thing which the Lord commanded, saying, Take ye from among you an offering unto the Lord: whosoever is of a willing heart, let him bring it, an offering of the Lord; gold, and silver, and brass."* (Exodus 35:3-5; see also Exodus 36:3-7; Haggai 1:3-15.)

WORSHIP OFFERING

Give unto the Lord the glory due unto his name: bring an offering, and come into his courts. O worship the Lord in the beauty of holiness: fear before him, all the earth.
Psalms 96:7-8

In the school of "DIVINE PROSPERITY it is a law to worship GOD with an offering. We owe GOD this ritual as our KINDGOM obligation. Our worship at every church service is incomplete unless we give an offering into the church basket.

We are commanded by the Holy Bible to not appear empty-handed in the presence of the ALMIGHTY GOD. *"Three times in a year shall all thy males appear before the Lord- thy God in the place which he shall choose; in the feast of unleavened bread, and in the feast of weeks, and in the feast of tabernacles: and they shall not appear before the Lord empty: Every man shall give as he is able, according to the blessing of the Lord thy God which he hath given thee."* (Deuteronomy 16:16-17)

> *Let them shout for joy, and be glad, that favour my righteous cause: yea, let them say continually, Let the Lord be magnified, which hath pleasure in the prosperity of his servant.*
> **Psalms 35:27**

This is because God takes cognizance of every offering we bring when we are in worship. (See Exodus 34:20; Proverbs 3:9-10; Mark 12:41-44.

IN SUMMARY

Our seed is not a financial donation to "HELP GOD," the church, the ministry or the pastor. Acknowledge that GOD is not in need and shall never be in need, even to the end of our lifetime here on Earth. Our giving is a spiritual channel to connect us with the blessing of the LORD.

UNDERSTANDING DIVINE PROPSERITY OPERATES ONLY ON THE PLATFORM OF THE COVENANT.

Lay not up for yourselves treasures upon earth, where moth and rust doth corrupt, and where thieves break through and steal: But lay up for yourselves treasures in heaven, where neither moth nor rust doth corrupt, and where thieves do not break through nor steal: For where your treasure is, there will your heart be also.
Matthew 6:19-21

As much as we desire material blessing, we must always put GOD first in all things in life. We must therefore set our heart RIGHT WITH GOD. GOD is the author and finisher of our FAITH. *"But seek ye first the kingdom of God, and his righteousness; and all these things shall be added unto you. Take therefore no thought for the morrow: for the morrow shall take thought for the things of itself. Sufficient unto the day is the evil thereof."* (Matthew 6:33)

We must therefore set our heart RIGHT WITH

GOD. GOD is the author and finisher of our FAITH. Our whole life will amount to nothing if we gain the whole world but lose our soul. *"For what shall it profit a man, if he shall gain the whole world, and lose his own soul? Or what shall a man give in exchange for his soul?"* (Mark 8:36-37)

CONCLUSION

Blessed is the man that feareth the Lord that delighteth greatly in his commandments. His seed shall be mighty upon earth: the generation of the upright shall be blessed. Wealth and riches shall be in his house: and his righteousness endureth forever.
Psalms 112:1-3

Without argument, "GIVING TO GOD" has remained a very sensitive and most widely criticized area of the church of JESUS CHRIST. DIVINE PROSPERITY does not answer to fasting. It has no respect for Prayers and Speaking in Tongue. You can be fire baptized to speak and preach in the Holy Ghost until your part of the covenant is played. GOD is not committed to prosper your life.

Let us hear the conclusion of the whole matter: Fear God, and keep his commandments: for this is the whole duty of man.
Ecclesiastes 12:13

To keep GOD's commandment, we must "GIVE IN ORDER FOR US to RECEIVE." UNDERSTANDING DIVINE PROSPERITY means understanding the binding kingdom fundamentals of GIVING AND RECIEVING. *"The liberal soul shall be made fat: and he that watereth shall be watered also himself."* (Proverbs 11:25)

For God shall bring every work into judgment,
with every secret thing, whether it be good,
or whether it be evil.
Ecclesiastes 12:14

All my grammar will not make any meaning, unless we commit it into practice. All I have said in this book will remain a story to you unless you are "born again." The Bible says in Ecclesiastes, *"For God shall bring every work into judgment, with every secret thing, whether it be good, or whether it be evil. If you are a born again Christian; we like to encourage you in your Christian life. If you are not a born again Christian we can help you here receive genuine salvation."* (Ecclesiastes 12:14)

Therefore if any man be in Christ, he is a new creature:
old things are passed away; behold, all things
are become new.
2 Corinthians 5:17

Now repeat this prayer after me:

Say Lord Jesus, I accept you today, as my Lord and my savior. Forgive me of my sins, wash me with your blood. Right now, I believe I am sanctified, I am saved, I am free. I am free from the power of sin, to serve the Lord Jesus. Thank you Lord for saving me. Amen.

Congratulations. You are now...

...a BORN AGAIN CHRISTIAN.

Again I say to you—CONGRATULATIONS!

What must I do to determine my divine visitation?

To determine divine visitation you must be born again! The word says as many as received him, to them gave He power to become the sons of God. Even to them that believe on his name.

To qualify for divine visitation, do the following sincerely:

1) Acknowledge that you are a sinner and that He died for you. (Romans 3:23)

2) Repent of your sins. (Acts 3:19, Luke 13:5, 2 Peter 3:9)

3) Believe in your heart that Jesus died for your sin. (Romans 10:10)

4) Confess Jesus as the Lord over your life.
(Romans 10:10, Acts 2:21)

NOW REPEAT THIS PRAYER AFTER ME:
Say Lord Jesus, I accept you today, as my Lord and my savior, forgive me of my sins wash me with your blood. Right now, I believe, I am sanctified, I am save, I am free, I am free from the Power of sin to serve the Lord Jesus. Thank you Lord for saving me. Amen.

Congratulations. You are now...

...a BORN AGAIN CHRISTIAN.

Again I say to you—CONGRATULATIONS!

I adjure you to watch the Spirit of God bear witness with your Spirit confirming His word with signs following. The word says The Spirit itself beareth witness with our spirit, that we are the children of God. Join a Bible-believing church or join us on our weekly and Sunday worship services at 343 Sanford Avenue Newark, New Jersey 07106.

HEALING KEYS

1) Always carry a positive mindset, regardless of the prevailing circumstances.

2) Always tell yourself the truth before you lie about it.

3) If the truth be told, you are a branch of His blessings, the planting of the Lord.

4) Never confess that you are sick to the hearing of the member of your body.

5) Positive confession with faith yields positive results.

6) Every cures of man have no power to prevail over your life.

7) A merry heart is medicinal and health to your body.

8) Spiritual and emotional well-being is vital to happiness in life.

9) To avoid depression, never have regrets.

10) Never be anxious in life to avoid anxiety.

11) Always live today for today to be at peace with your spirit and with God.

12) You're unique because your challenges are tailored to you only.

13) The blessing always dominates the curses any day.

14) Decisions are the wheels of life.

15) We either ride into fame or into shame.

16) Daily exercise and some reading of the Bible gurantees good health.

17) Every day is God's day. No day created by God is a disapointment.

18) Stay away from sweet stuff—they are temporary.

19) Sugar is sweet to your taste, beware! It also contributes to diabetes.

20) A good prayer life gurantees longivity.

21) People that pray in tongues do not develop mental disease.

22) Always be positive in everything.

23) Always have a mentor in life that will oppose and fight the tormentor.

24) Always have someone in life to learn from.

25) Tell everybody what you plan to do and someone will help you do it.

26) Winners fight to the last.

27) Quitters never win in life.

28) Soul winners are heirs to the kingdom of god.

29) Soul winners never lack help.

30) Soul winners are cerified with divine help.

31) God is always looking for soul winners to bless.

32) Life is a warfare and not a funfare.

33) In life you fight for all you possess.

34) No man or woman was born rich.

35) In your lifetime do something positive to impact your world.

36) Take care of your life today—you don't have one to spare.

37) Take your life serious before the devil take you down.

38) Always be cheerful at all times.

39) Regardless of the prevailing circumstances around you, your life is in the hand of God.

40) God is the super surgeon that will spiritually-surgically heal you.

41) Always expect help from above and not from abroad.

42) Man will disappoint you, but god will appoint you.

43) The joy of the lord is always our strength.

44) Spiritual height is not measured in length or breath.

45) If you go deeper with God, you will see deeper.

46) Your next level in life is full of recognition.

47) Go to where you are celebrated and not where you are tolerated.

48) Develop yourself in the area of your calling in life.

49) A lifestyle of thanks given keeps God 24/7 on duty on our behalf.

50) Develop a lifestyle of thanksgiving.

51) Thanksgiving guarantees our access to obtain the promises.

WISDOM KEYS

— Every productive society is a society heading to the top.

—Millions of Nigerians run away from Nigeria. Very few Nigerians stay in Nigeria.

—My decision to return Nigeria is the will of God for my life.

—My shortcoming in America after 18 years is the fact that I've trained me to be wise, to think, reflect and reason appropriately.

—If you train your mind to reason, it will train your hands to earn money.

—It is absurd to use the money of the heathen to build the kingdom of the living God.

—Every ministry reveals its agenda and VISION either at the beginning or at the end.

—Be careful of your life. It is your first ministry.

—The average American mind is conditioned for a continual quest to get new things and discard the old.

—When I considered well, my BMW jeep became my initial deposit for the work of the ministry in Nigeria.

—Money will never fall from any tree or person. Make up your mind to be independent today.

—Everyone is waiting for you to change your mind. Until you change your thinking, nothing changes around you.

—Multiple academic degrees in other disciplines gave me the chance to think and reason.

—Whatever anyone is thinking at any time reveals what is inside of their heart.

—All planned events are the product of meditation.

—Every event is designed for a designated timeline.

—Wisdom is your ability to think, to create and invent.

— If you can think wisely enough, you will come out of debt.

—The distance between you and your success is your innovative and creative ability to think well.

—Success is the result of hard work, commitment, resolve and determined learning from past mistakes and failings.

—If you organize your mind, you have organized your life and destiny.

—There is a thin line between success and failure.

—Wealth is your ability to think, power is your ability to reason and success is your ability to be informed.

—If you can make use of your mind by thinking and reasoning, God will make use of your life and destiny.

—Reflect, reason, think and be Great.

—Famous people are born of woman.

—That you will make it is your intention, that you will survive is your resolve, that you will succeed with changes is your determination, personal efforts and hard work.

—No man was born a failure.

—Lack of vision is the result of failure.

—Working with mental patients encourages and aspire me to be a productive observant and dedicated to my assignment.

—Successful people are not magicians. It is the will-power, combined with hard work and determination and a resolve to succeed, that make them succeed.

—In the unequivocal state of the mind, intention is not a location or a position. It is the state of the mind.

—So many people think that they think.

—The mind is used to think, to reflect and to reason.

—You will remain blind with your eyes open until you can see with your mind by thinking.

—There is no favoritism in accurate and precise calculation.

—Although knowledge is power, information is the key and gateway to a great future.

—It will take the hand of God to move the hand of man.

—With the backing of the great wise God, nothing will disconnect you from your inheritance.

—As long as you have wisdom and understanding of God, Satan and evil cannot manipulate your life and destiny.

—You have come this far in life by your own judgment and the decisions you made in the past. Now lean in and listen to God for another dimension of greatness.

—Great people are ordinary people. It is extra ordinary efforts and the price of sacrifice that produces greatness in them.

—As a mental direct care worker, I saw a great pastor and a motivational speaker within myself.

—A menial job does not reduce your self-worth. Until you resolve to achieve greatness and see greatness in all you do, you will never count in your community.

—The principle of Jesus will solve your gambling and addiction problems.

—The man of Jesus will lead you into heaven.

—Everyone has their self-appraisal and what they think about you. Until you discover yourself, other opinions about you will alter the real you.

—Supervisors and directors are just a position in the chain of command in a workplace. Never allow your supervisor hierarchy to alter your opinion of yourself.

—Everyone can come out of debt if they make up their mind.

—The fact that I am not a decision-maker at work does not diminish my contribution to my world.

—Although it appears like it was a poor decision to accept a direct care employment at a psychiatric hospital, as I reflect on my nine years of that experience, it became apparent that I have learned and experienced enough for my next assignment.

—Self-encouragement and determination is a resolve of the heart.

—If you are determined to make a difference and do the things that make a difference, you will eventually make a difference.

—Good things do not come easy.

—Short cuts will cut your life short.

—Those who look ahead move ahead.

—Life is all about making an impact. In your lifetime strive to make an impact in your community.

—Make friends and connect with people who are moving ahead of you in life.

—If you can look around well, you have come a long way in your life, made a lot of difference and realized a lot of success in life.
—If you are my old friend, hurry up to reach out to me before I become a stranger to you.

—I am blessed with inspirations from God that changed my interpretation of the world around me.

—I thought I was stagnant and lonely until I looked around and noticed my children running around and my wife cooking.

— At 40, I resigned my job to seek the Lord forever.

—My ministry took a drastic rise to the top when the wisdom of God visited me with knowledge and understanding.

—You will be a better person if you understand the characteristics of your personality like your mood swings, attitudes and habits.

—It is the seed of love you sow into the heart of a child and a woman that you reap in due time.

—Love is not selfish. Love shares everything, including the concealed secrets of the mind.

—As long as you have a prayer life and a Bible, you will never feel lonely in the race of life.

—When good friends disconnect from you, let them go. They might have seen something new in a different direction.

—Confidence in yourself and in God is the only way to bring you out of captivity

—Never train a child to waste his or her time.

—The mind is the greatest asset of a great future.

—You walk by common sense, run by principles and fly by instruction.

—Those who become successful in life did it by self-determination, hard work and learning from past failures.

—Most successful people are lonely people. No one renders help to them, believing they are already successful. Except when they seek for more knowledge and information, they are all alone.

— I have seen a towing truck vehicle. I have also seen a towing ship in the water. But I have never seen a towing airplane in the air.

—I exercise my judgment and make a decision every minute of the day. Decisions are crucial, critical and vital with reference to your future.

—So many people wish for a great future. You can only work towards a great future.

—Your celebrity status began when you discovered your talent. What are you good at? Work at it with all your commitment.

—Prayers will sustain you, but the wisdom of God will prosper you.

—When I met Oyedepo, his teachings changed my perspective. But when I met Ibiyeomie, his teachings changed my perception.

— I will be successful in ministry if only I concentrate and focus my energy in the work of the ministry.

— It took the late Dr. Norman Vincent Peale's book to open my mind towards the kingdom of success.

CHAPTER 4
PRAYER OF SALVATION

I am glad you have read this book all the way from the beginning to this point. All I have said from the beginning will remain a mystery until you commit it into practice.

And before you do so, I want you—if you have not given your life to Jesus already—to do so now. Give your life to Christ. I want you to know the truth! The truth is that Jesus died for your sins and because He died, you must be alive and prosperous.

What must I do to determine my divine visitation?

To determine divine visitation, you must be born again! The word says, *"As many as received Him, to them gave He power to become the sons of God. Even to them that believe on his name."* (John 1:12)

To qualify for divine visitation, do the following with sincerity—

1) Acknowledge that you are a sinner and that He died for you. (Romans 3:23)
2) Repent of your sins. (Acts 3:19, Luke 13:5, 2 Peter 3:9)
3) Believe in your heart that Jesus died for your sins. (Romans 10:10)

4) Confess Jesus as the Lord over your life.
(Romans 10:10, Acts 2:21)

Now repeat this prayer after me:

Say Lord Jesus, I accept you today, as my Lord and my savior. Forgive me of my sins, wash me with your blood. Right now, I believe I am sanctified, I am saved, I am free. I am free from the power of sin, to serve the Lord Jesus. Thank you Lord for saving me. Amen.

Congratulations. You are now...

A BORN AGAIN CHRISTIAN.

Again I say to you—CONGRATULATIONS!

I adjure you to watch the Spirit of God bear witness with your Spirit, confirming His word with subsequent signs. The word says, *"The Spirit itself beareth witness with our spirit, that we are the children of God."* (Romans 8:16)

MIRACLE CARE OUTREACH

"...But that the members should have the same care one for another"
1 Corinthians 12:25

We are all members of the body of Christ. Jesus commanded us to love our neighbor as ourselves. This includes caring for one another as a member of one body. True love is expressed in caring and giving. The word says, for God so Love He gave....

Reach out to someone in need of Jesus. Help someone in crisis find Christ. Look out and prove your love to Jesus by caring and inviting your friends and associates to find Jesus the Healer.

Invite your friends to our Home Care Cell Fellowship (Miracle Chapel Intl. Satellite Fellowship). We're in the U.S. at 33 Schley Street, Newark, New Jersey 07112. Home Care Cell Fellowship Group meets every Tuesday at 6:00pm-7:00pm.

If you are in Nigeria—MIRACLE OF GOD MINISTRIES, aka "MIRACLE CHAPEL INTL." Mpama–Egbu-Owerri Imo state Nigeria.

LIFE IS NOT ALL ABOUT DURATION, BUT IT'S ALL ABOUT DONATION

What does this statement mean?
Life consists not in accumulation of material

wealth. (Luke 12:15) But it's all about liberality...i.e., what you can give and share with others. (Proverbs 11:25) When you live for others, you live forever—because you outlive your generation by the legacy you leave behind after you depart into glory to be with the Lord. But when you live for yourself, when you are reduced to SELF—you are easily forgotten when you die and depart in glory.

Permit me to admonish you today to live your life to be a blessing to a soul connected to you today. I want you to know that so many souls are connected and looking up to you, and through you so many souls will be saved and rescued from destruction. Will you disciple someone today to find Jesus Christ?

As a genuine Christian, it is your duty to evangelize Jesus Christ to all you meet on your way. Jesus is still in the healing business—Jesus is still doing miracles, from time of old to now. Therefore, tell someone about Jesus Christ today, disciple and bring them to Church. *Philip findeth Nathanael...* (John 1:45)

Please prove the sincerity of your love for God today, please become a soul winner. The dignity of your Christianity is hidden in your boldness to proclaim and evangelize Jesus Christ to all you meet on your way. There is a question mark on the integrity of your Christianity until you become a life soul winner. Invite someone to join us worship the Lord Jesus this coming Sunday. Amen.

MIRACLE OF GOD MINISTRIES
PILLARS OF THE COMMISSION

We Believe, Preach and Practice the following:

1) We believe and preach Salvation to every living human being.

2) We believe and preach Repentance and Forgiveness of sins.

3) We believe and preach the baptism of the Holy Spirit and Spiritual gifts.

4) We believe and teach Prosperity.

5) We believe and preach Divine Healing and Miracles—Signs and Wonder.

6) We believe and preach Faith.

7) We believe and proclaim the Power of God (Supernatural).

8) We believe and proclaim Praise and Worship to God.

9) We believe and preach Wisdom.

10) We believe and preach Holiness (Consecration).

11) We believe and preach Vision.

12) We believe and teach the Word of God.

13) We believe and teach Success.

14) We believe and practice Prayer.

15) We believe and teach Deliverance.

These 15 stones form the Pillars of Our Commission. Become part of this church family and follow this great move of God.

MY HEARTFELT PRAYER FOR YOU

It is my burning desire for God to touch you through one of our teaching books or CDs. It also my personal desire for you encounter God for yourself.

Now let me Pray for you:

I plead the precious blood of Jesus over your life. I decree and declare that no weapon fashioned against you shall ever prosper, every tongue that shall rise up against you God shall condemn it in judgement. From this day I declare your name in the lamb book of life. From this great day I declare goodness and mercy to hunt you down all the days of your life. Remain blessed, in Jesus name. Amen.

HIS DESTINY WAS THE CROSS....

HIS PURPOSE WAS LOVE....

HIS REASON WAS YOU....

For God so loved the world, that he gave his only begotten Son, that whosoever believeth in him should not perish, but have everlasting life.
John 3:16

THE WHOLE ESSENCE OF LIFE

"Life is a story. We must write our story with a noble pen." You will not be here forever. Therefore, invest your time wisely and productively. Every time you live for others, you will live forever. But when you live only to your self alone, you are reduced to self.

Oftentimes most of us make a big deal out of life circumstances. We easily magnify our problems and even curse GOD. With all the calamity that happened to Job in the Bible, the Bible said Job did not sin. *"In all this Job sinned not, nor charged God foolishly."* (Job 1:22) We easily get anxious, angry and irritated over things that really do not matter. I have seen people commit suicide for no good reason. We must always have this consciousness that we cannot create any life. *"The Lord gave, and the Lord hath taken away; blessed be the name of the Lord."* (Job 1:20)

In our lifetime, we must make a difference— not only with our family members, but we must also impact the people that are around us. Our lives must reflect a life full of thanksgiving, a life we all can emulate from, a life just like our master Jesus.

Every man also to whom God hath given
riches and wealth, and hath given him power
to eat thereof, and to take his portion,
and to rejoice in his labour; this is the gift of God.
For he shall not much remember the days of his life;
because God answereth him in the joy of his heart.
Ecclesiastes 5:19-20

It is written, *"For whom he did foreknow, he also did predestinate to be conformed to the image of his Son, that he might be the firstborn among many brethren."* (Romans 8:29)

GOD CREATED US TO REFLECT HIS GLORY

We must command covenant wealth as a peculiar people of GOD. *"But ye are a chosen generation, a royal priesthood, an holy nation, a peculiar people; that ye should shew forth the praises of him who hath called you out of darkness into his marvellous light."* (1 Peter 2:9)

"Moreover whom he did predestinate, them he also called: and whom he called, them he also justified: and whom he justified, them he also glorified." (Romans 8:30)

WE WERE CREATED IN THE IMAGE OF GOD

We must all live our lives for God, we must always work towards perfection, fulfilling the plan and purpose of God in our lives.

NO MAN OR WOMAN WAS BORN A DESTITUTE OR A CURSE

As far as I am concerned, you are a symbol of His blessing. You may not have all the wealth to give a million dollars to charity, but only a perfect heart is what the Lord Jesus Christ is looking for.

Remember...

The sacrifices of God are a broken spirit: a broken and a contrite heart, O God, thou wilt not despise. Do good in thy good pleasure unto Zion: build thou the walls of Jerusalem.
Psalms 51:17-18

REFLECTION FOR THE RICH

Charge them that are rich in this world, that they be not highminded, nor trust in uncertain riches, but in the living God, who giveth us richly all things to enjoy; That they do good, that they be rich in good works, ready to distribute, willing to communicate; Laying up in store for themselves a good foundation against the time to come, that they may lay hold on eternal life.
1 Timothy 6:17-19

RICH MEN AND WOMEN MUST BE HUMBLED PEOPLE.

TIME TO TURN TO GOD

Every rich person must be humbled and must LOVE THE KINGDOM OF GOD AND HIS RIGHTEOUSNESS. *"And again I say unto you, It is easier for a camel to go through the eye of a needle, than for a rich man to enter into the kingdom of God."* (Matthew 19:24)

WHAT SHALL A MAN GIVE IN EXCHANGE FOR HIS SOUL?

BE CAUTIOUS!—BEWARE!—BE WARNED!!

MONEY WILL NOT BUY US A TICKET INTO HEAVEN. YOUR SOUL IS VERY IMPORATANT TO JESUS CHRIST.

"For what shall it profit a man, if he shall gain the whole world, and lose his own soul? Or what shall a man give in exchange for his soul?" (Mark 8:36-37)

Eternity is real. Heaven is sure. Hell is inevitable.

Eternity is inevitable, therefore we must make genuine plans to make it in heaven. In your lifetime, strive to live a life of contentment, full of joy, honor, humility and respect—a life worthy for others to emulate morally and spiritually. *"But godliness with contentment is great gain."* (1 Timothy 6:6)

ABOUT THE AUTHOR

Rev. Franklin N. Abazie is the founding and Presiding Pastor of Miracle of God Ministries, with headquarters in Newark, New Jersey USA and a branch church in Owerri-Imo State Nigeria. He is following the footsteps of one of his mentors, the healing evangelist Oral Roberts of the blessed memory. The Lord passed Oral Roberts' healing mantle two days before he went to be with the Lord at age 91 into the hands of healing evangelist Rev. Franklin N. Abazie in a vision.

In all his services, the Power and Presence of God is present to heal all in his audience. Rev. Abazie is an ordained man of God, with a Healing Ministry reviving the healing and miracle ministry of Jesus Christ of Nazareth.

Pastor Franklin N. Abazie, has been called by God with a unique mandate: **"THE MOMENT IS DUE TO IMPACT YOUR WORLD THROUGH THE REVIVAL OF THE HEALING AND MIRACLE MINISTRY OF JESUS CHRIST OF NAZARETH.**

"I AM SENDING YOU TO RESTORE HEALTH UNTO THEE AND I WILL HEAL THEE OF THY WOUNDS, SAID THE LORD OF HOST."

Rev. Abazie is a gifted, ardent teacher of the word of God, who operates also in the office of a

Prophet, generating and attracting undeniable signs and wonders, special miracles and healings, with apostolic fireworks of the Holy Ghost. He is the founding and presiding senior Pastor of this fast growing Healing Ministry. He has written over 86 inspirational, healing and transforming books covering almost all aspects of divine healing and life. He is happily married and blessed with children.

BOOKS BY REV. FRANKLIN N. ABAZIE:

1) The Outcome of Faith
2) Understanding the Secret of Prevailing Prayers
3) Commanding Abundance
4) Understanding the Secret of the Man God Uses
5) Activating My Due Season
6) Overcoming Divine Verdicts
7) The Outcome of Divine Wisdom
8) Understanding God's Restoration Mandate
9) Walking In the Victory and Authority of the Truth
10) God's Covenant Exemption
11) Destiny Restoration Pillars
12) Provoking Acceptable Praise
13) Understanding Divine Judgment
14) Activating Angelic Re-enforcement
15) Provoking Un-Merited Favo
16) The Benefits of the Speaking Faith
17) Understanding Divine Arrangement
18) How to Keep Your Healing
19) Understanding the Mysteries of the Speaking Faith
20) Understanding the Mysteries of Prophetic Healing
21) Operating Under the Rules of Creative Healing
22) Understanding the Joy of Breakthrough
23) Understanding the Mystery of Breakthrough
24) Understanding Divine Prosperity
25) Understanding Divine Healing
26) Retaining Your Inheritance
27) Overcoming Confusing Spirit
28) Commanding Angelic Escorts

29) Enforcing Your Inheritance In Christ Jesus
30) Understanding Your Guardian Angels
31) Overcoming the Dominion of Sin
32) Understanding the Voice of God
33) The Outstanding Benefits of the Anointing
34) The Audacity of the Blood of Jesus
35) Walking in the Reality of the Anointing
36) Escaping the Nightmare of Poverty
37) Understanding Your Harvest Season
38) Activating Your Success Buttons
39) Overcoming the Forces of Darkness
40) Overcoming the Devices of the Devil
41) Overcoming Demonic Agents
42) Overcoming the Sorrows of Failure
43) Rejecting the Sorrows of Failure
44) Resisting the Sorrows of Poverty
45) Restoring Broken Marriages
46) Redeeming Your Days
47) The Force of Vision
48) Overcoming the Forces of Ignorance
49) Understanding the Sacrifice of Small Beginning
50) The Might of Small Beginning
51) Understanding the Mysteries of Prophesy
52) Overcoming Dream Nightmares
53) Breaking the Shackles of the Curse of the Law
54) Understanding the Joy of Harvest
55) Wisdom for Signs & Wonders
56) Wisdom for Generational Impact
57) Wisdom for Marriage Stability
58) Understanding the Number of Your Days

59) Enforcing Your Kingdom Rights
60) Escaping the Traps of Immoralities
61) Escaping the Trap of Poverty
62) Accessing Biblical Prosperity
63) Accessing True Riches in Christ
64) Silencing the Voice of the Accuser
65) Overcoming the Forces of Oppositions
66) Quenching the Voice of the Avenger
67) Silencing Demonic Prediction & Projection
68) Silencing Your Mocker
69) Understanding the Power of the Holy Ghost
70) Understanding the Baptism of Power
71) The Mystery of the Blood of Jesus
72) Understanding the Mystery of Sanctification
73) Understanding the Power of Holiness
74) Understanding the Forces of Purity & Righteousness
75) Activating the Forces of Vengeance
76) Appreciating the Mystery of Restoration
77) Overcoming the Projection & Prediction of the Enemy
78) Engaging the Mystery of the Blood
79) Commanding the Power of the Speaking Faith
80) Uprooting the Forces Against Your Rising
81) Overcoming Mere Success Syndrome
82) Understanding Divine Sentence
83) Understanding the Mystery of Praise
84) Understanding the Author of Faith
85) The Mystery of the Finisher of Faith
86) Attracting Supernatural Favor

MIRACLE OF GOD MINISTRIES
NIGERIA CRUSADE
2012

MIRACLE OF GOD MINISTRIES
NIGERIA CRUSADE 2012

MIRACLE OF GOD MINISTRIES

NIGERIA CRUSADE

2012

MIRACLE OF GOD MINISTRIES

NIGERIA CRUSADE

2012

MIRACLE OF GOD MINISTRIES

NIGERIA CRUSADE 2012

www.ingramcontent.com/pod-product-compliance
Lightning Source LLC
Chambersburg PA
CBHW021445080526
44588CB00009B/703